The kite contest

Story written by Karra McFarlane
Illustrated by Tim Archbold

Speed Sounds

Ask your child to say the sounds (not the letter names) clearly and quickly, in and out of order. Make sure he or she does not add 'uh' to the end of the sounds, e.g. 'f' not 'fuh'.

Each box contains one sound. Focus sounds for this story are circled.

Consonants

f	l	m	n	r	s	v	z	sh	th	ng
ff	ll	mm	nn	rr	ss	**ve**	zz			nk
ph	le	mb	**kn**	wr	se		se			
			gn		**c**		s			
					ce					

b	c	d	g	h	j	p	qu	t	w	x	y	ch
bb	k	dd	gg		g	pp		tt	**wh**			tch
	ck		gu		ge							
					dge							

Vowels

Ask your child to say the sounds in and out of order.

a	e	i	o	u	ay	ee	igh	ow
	ea				a-e	ea	i-e	o-e
					a	y	ie	o
						e	i	oe
at	h**e**n	**i**n	**o**n	**u**p	d**ay**	s**ee**	h**igh**	bl**ow**

oo	oo	ar	or	air	ir	ou	oy
u-e			oor	are	ur	ow	oi
ue			ore		er		
			aw				
z**oo**	l**oo**k	c**ar**	f**or**	f**air**	wh**ir**l	sh**ou**t	b**oy**

Story Green Words

For each word ask your child to read the separate sounds, e.g. 'b-u-s', 'p-oo-l' and then blend sounds together to make the word, e.g. 'bus', 'pool'. Sometimes one sound is represented by more than one letter, e.g. 'th', 'oo'. These are underlined.

Miss Knight prize gust flung tied sight goes

Ask your child to say the syllables and then read the whole word.

Nad|in yell|ow chil|dren con|test sudd|en con|fi|dent play|ground

Ask your child to read the root first and then the whole word with the suffix.

tight → tightly mate → mates reveal → revealed

compete → competing arrive → arrived tug → tugged

excite → excited high → higher hold → holding*

** Challenge Words*

Vocabulary Check

Tell your child the meaning of each word in the context of the story.

	definition:	**sentence:**
gust	*rush*	*... a sudden gust of wind tugged the kite from his hands...*
smirked	*smiled in a mean way*	*"You lost your kite!" Nadin smirked.*
flung	*threw something hard*	*He flung the kite into the air...*
revealed	*told them something they didn't know*	*... Miss Knight revealed the team that had scooped the prize.*
scooped	*won*	*... Miss Knight revealed the team that had scooped the prize.*

Red Words

Red words don't sound like they look. Ask your child to read the words but if he or she gets stuck read the word to your child.

one	school	my	other
your	some	all	could
old	through	son	anyone
water	were	their	does
want	put	would	over

The kite contest

Do not read the story to your child first. Point to the words as your child reads. If your child gets stuck on a word help him or her say the sounds and blend them together. Re-read each sentence to your child to help him or her remember what he or she has read. Discuss what is happening on each page.

Ash and Nadin were best mates, but they liked competing with each other. Sometimes Ash would win and sometimes Nadin would win. They didn't do things for fun. They did things to win!

One morning, Miss Knight told the children there was going to be a kite contest at school.

"You have a week to make your kites," she said. "You can team up if you want to or you can make your kite on your own. There will be a prize for the kite that gets the highest."

Ash and Nadin were excited about the contest. Ash really wanted to win... and so did Nadin. They didn't like being a team so they decided to make their own kites.

Ash made a bright green kite with red ribbons tied to the string. He took the kite to the park to test it out with his dad. He felt confident he was going to win the prize!

Nadin made a white kite with yellow ribbons. He spent lots of time putting the ribbons on the string. He felt confident *he* was going to win the prize!

On the day of the contest, Ash and Nadin arrived first. The playground filled up with children holding kites, and the contest began.

Ash started off well and led his kite up and up, high into the air. But then a sudden gust of wind tugged the kite from his hands and it crashed into a tree!

"You lost your kite!" Nadin smirked, but then he started to feel bad.
"Let's pair up," Nadin said. "You can help with my kite if you like."

Ash was grateful he was still in the contest.
"Thanks, let's go!" he cried.

He flung the kite into the air as Nadin ran, holding tightly to the string. They made a good team. The kite went quickly up into the air. The strong wind took the kite higher and higher. The boys got their kite so high that it disappeared from sight!

When the contest finished, Miss Knight revealed the team that had scooped the prize.

"It was very close... but the prize for the highest kite goes to... Ash and Nadin."

All the children clapped. Ash and Nadin jumped with joy. They had teamed up, enjoyed themselves *and* collected the prize!

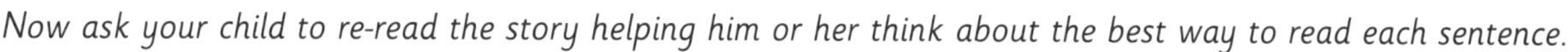

Now ask your child to re-read the story helping him or her think about the best way to read each sentence.

Questions to talk about

Read the questions aloud to your child and ask him or her to find the answers on the relevant pages. Do not ask your child to read the questions – the words are harder than he or she can read at the moment.

p.10	Who told the children about the kite contest?
p.11	Ash and Nadin are best mates. Did they want to work together?
pp.11–12	Which boy tried hardest to make his kite?
p.13	What happened to Ash's kite?
p.14	Why did Nadin let Ash help him?
p.15	How did Ash and Nadin win the contest?

Questions to read and answer

Ask your child to read the questions and find the correct answer in the story.

1. The children had **a day / three weeks / a week** to make their kites.

2. Ash's kite was bright green with **red / yellow / black** ribbons.

3. Nadin was confident **Ash / Miss Knight / he** was going to win.

4. Ash and Nadin teamed up as **they liked being a team / Ash's kite crashed / Miss Knight asked them to team up**.

5. Ash and Nadin's kite was the **highest / biggest / brightest**.

Speedy Green Words

Ask your child to read the words clearly and quickly – across the rows, down the columns, and in and out of order.

time	like	make	string
green	started	took	pair
day	each	park	tree
kite	for	air	first
boys	own	white	morning